WHY DOES GOD ALLOW SUFFERING AND EVIL?

CONTENDERS BIBLE STUDY SERIES™

JOHN ANKERBERG

DILLON BURROUGHS

Advancing the Ministries of the Gospel

AMG *Publishers*

God's Word to you is our highest calling.

Contenders Bible Study Series

Why Does God Allow Suffering and Evil?

First Printing, May 2008
ISBN 13: 978-089957-782-1

Editing by Rick Steele and Christy Graeber

Layout by PerfecType, Nashville, Tennessee

Cover Design by Indoor Graphics Corp., Chattanooga, Tennessee

Printed in Canada
13 12 11 10 09 08 –T– 6 5 4 3 2 1

Table of Contents

Session 6:

Foreword

By Dr. Norman Geisler

When Jude wrote his New Testament letter to Christians in the early church he felt compelled to urge his readers to "contend for the faith" (Jude 3). His words continue to provide a strong motivation for us today to understand the reasons behind what we believe both for our own personal growth and in order to communicate our faith to others.

The Contenders series of Bible study books by John Ankerberg and Dillon Burroughs is designed to provide a response for this tremendous need. As followers of Christ, we are instructed to be prepared to share the reason for our hope (1 Peter 3:15). In addition, those still seeking the truth regarding Jesus and the Word of God are encouraged, as the hearers of Paul in Berea were, to examine the Scriptures to discover if what they had been taught was true (Acts 17:11).

The innovative material found in this series can assist you in two specific ways. First, if you are already a believer in Christ, this series can provide answers to many of the complex questions you may be facing—or that you are asking yourself. Second, if you are a skeptic or seeker of spiritual truth contemplating what it means to follow Jesus Christ, this series can also help provide a factual basis for the Christian faith and the questions in your quest. You can feel free to wrestle with the difficult issues of the Christian faith in the context of friendly conversation with others. This is a powerful tool for individuals who sincerely desire to learn more about God and the amazing truths given to us in the Bible.

If you are one of the people who have chosen to participate in this new series, I applaud your efforts to grow in spiritual truth. Let the pages of this resource provide the basis for your journey as you learn more about contending for the faith we communicate in Jesus Christ.

Dr. Norman Geisler,
co-founder of Southern Evangelical Seminary
and author of seventy books, including the award-winning
Baker Encyclopedia of Christian Apologetics

Introduction

Welcome to the Contenders series! This small-group curriculum was developed with the conviction that claims about today's spiritual issues can and should be investigated. Christianity, sometimes stereotyped as non-intellectual and uneducated, is not allowed to make assertions of faith without providing practical answers why it should be taken seriously. If the Bible claims to be God's Word and claims to provide explanations for the most significant issues of life, both now and eternally, these assertions should be carefully examined. If this investigation proves these beliefs flawed, the only reasonable choice is to refuse to follow the Christian Scriptures as truth. However, if our investigation of the evidence leads to the discovery of truth, then the search will have been worthwhile. In fact, it will be life-changing.

Christians understand that God welcomes sincere seekers of truth. In fact, Jesus Christ Himself openly cheered such inquiry. The Bible is not a book shrouded in mystery, open to only a select group of experts. It is widely available for discussion and learning by anyone. The core beliefs of Christianity are publicly presented to anyone willing to consider their truths, whether skeptic, seeker, or life-long believer.

Consider this book your invitation. Investigate the choices, analyze the beliefs, and make your decisions. But be prepared—the truth you encounter is not another file to simply add to your collection. The truth of God's Word will transform every area of your life.

We often learn that we have mistakenly believed something that turns out to be false. We may even find ourselves not wanting to accept truth because it infringes upon our lifestyle or conflicts with long-held personal values. Through this series of discussion questions we will journey together to answer the question Pilate asked Jesus long ago: "What is truth?" (John 18:38). As authors, it is our hope that you will ultimately come to realize that Christian faith is based upon solid evidence worthy to build one's life upon. Whether you are currently still building your opinions on spiritual issues or are already a follower of Christ developing answers for your own questions and the questions of others, these guides will assist you on a captivating exploration of spiritual issues necessary in order to "contend for the faith" (Jude 3).

The Contenders Series for Your Group

The Contenders series is purposely designed to give truth seekers (those still investigating a relationship with Christ) an opportunity to ask questions and probe into the basics of Christianity within the friendly, caring environment of small-group discussion—typically in a group no larger than about a dozen people, with one or two individuals who serve as the discussion leaders. These leaders are responsible to coordinate the regular gatherings, build relationships with group members, and prepare to ask and answer questions, involving each person in the discussion. Through a combination of caring friendships, intelligent conversations, and genuine spiritual interest, it is our hope that these discussions will provide the basis for a fresh approach to exploring key concepts of Christian belief.

Because one of the intentions of this series is to address the real questions of the spiritual seeker, the questions are presented to represent the viewpoints of both the Christian and the skeptic. While the truths of Christianity are explicitly affirmed, hopefully many who join these discussions will find their own viewpoints understood and represented along the way. As seekers and skeptics feel valued in their current beliefs, they will be more open to honest discussion that leads to truth. The ultimate hope behind the Contenders series is that many who are seeking will come to know the truth about Christ, and that those who already follow Jesus will understand how to address the issues of their friends who are still exploring Christianity.

Of course, it is also important that those who already follow Jesus learn to grow in the basic beliefs of the Christian faith. As they do so, it will become easier to communicate the good news of the Christian faith in normal, everyday conversations with co-workers, neighbors, classmates, relatives, and even complete strangers. The process of struggling through these important issues and difficult questions will not only enhance one's own personal growth but also provide many specific details that can be used in everyday scenarios when the topic of faith arises with others.

Many groups will consist of some blend of believers and seekers. For example, your church may use this material for one of its small groups that consists mostly of people who already follow Christ. However, in the process, group members should feel comfortable and even encouraged to invite friends who have yet to begin a relationship with Christ. Special events designed to invite friends from outside of your current group, including simple social opportunities like dinner parties, a game night, movie night, or other activity should be considered. Regardless of the specific options selected, we pray that you will benefit tremendously as you use these guides to connect through interactive discussions about the issues of ultimate importance.

How to Use This Guide

Getting Started

At the start of each session is a segment of introductory material, typically several paragraphs in length. Each participant will want to read this information before the session begins, even if it is read again when the group is together. This "Getting Started" section is written with the skeptic in mind, often including very controversial perspectives to stimulate challenging discussion. As a result, each person should instantly feel the ability to share his or her viewpoint within the safe context of a caring group of friends.

Talk about It

Next, each session includes a range of ten to twenty questions your group can use during discussion. Most groups will find it impossible to use every single question every time. The options are either to choose which questions best fit the needs of your group, or to use the questions for more than one time together. The key component of this "Talk about It" section is to include each and every person, allowing the conversation to help people process their thoughts on the issue.

Often, the opening question of each session is a simple opinion question. Through the use of this ice-breaker approach, the conversation quickly takes off as each person offers his or her thoughts on a non-threatening issue that touches on the topic of the particular session. Certainly, the creativity of the group may also provide additional or alternative ice-breaker questions or activities to start each session. The goal is to achieve quick and enjoyable involvement by everyone in the group.

Here's What I'm Thinking

The next section, called "Here's What I'm Thinking," transitions the time of discussion toward a more emotional element. The questions in this section deal directly with personal responses to the material in each session rather than just intellectual facts or opinions. This is a time to communicate what each person is feeling about the topic, since this is a critical step in helping a person come to a personal decision about the issue.

What Now?

In the "What Now?" section, participants are challenged to move beyond both intellectual and emotional responses toward personal application of the material shared in the session. Once each person has considered his or her personal position on the issue, the next part of the process is to determine how this position influences daily living. One interesting impact of this section is that each person will begin to understand the implications of both true and faulty beliefs, along with charting personal changes in belief formation from one session to the next.

Consider This

Each session also includes one or more segments called "Consider This," designed to provide additional factual material appropriate to each discussion. Each "Consider This" section is immediately followed by a question based on the material, so it's important (especially for leaders) to read and understand this part before each meeting.

What Others Have Said

Throughout each session, participants will discover various quotes on the topic of discussion. Rather than quoting primarily academic sources, these quotes provide diverse perspectives from those critical of the Christian faith and well-known personalities from today's culture, along with well-worded thoughts from some of today's top writers.

Additional Resources

At the end of each guide, we have provided a list of several resources from the authors on the issue. This is only an introduction to a vast array of print, audio, video, and electronic materials based on decades of research in these areas.

A Word to Discussion Leaders

One distinctive feature of the Contenders series is that the learning does not end with the material found in this book. The series website www.contendersseries.com is loaded with interactive links to numerous online articles, outside internet links, video clips, audio responses, and creative ways to help direct the discussions in your group. We hope you'll also find it to be an excellent personal study source as well. And if you still don't find the answer you're looking for, or just want to connect with the authors of this resource, you'll find a place where you can email your questions and other feedback for personal responses.

Creating Boundaries

These guides consist mostly of questions for one reason—they are intended to spark conversation rather than fill-in-the-blank answers. In one sense, these discussions are not conventional Bible studies, though they often refer to Bible verses and biblical themes. Instead, consider these sessions as study guides, designed to assist participants in discussing what they feel and think on important spiritual issues.

Each topic is developed around a central point and clear conclusion, but they leave much of the "middle" open to the thoughts of those involved in the discussion. Every person brings perspectives, past experiences, and personal questions to the group. Rather than suppress these individual contributions, each session seeks to draw out the thoughts of each person, comparing the thinking of those in the group with what the Bible communicates in order to point members toward spiritual growth.

Much of the group's success will be determined by its leader(s). Those coordinating the group can also find additional material for each session at the Contenders series website at www.contendersseries.com. At the website, leader(s) will find suggested articles, additional facts, and suggested answers for many of the questions in each session. (Individual participants in your group are welcome to use these resources as well.) In addition, a personal daily study in the AMG Following God™ series called *Defending Your Faith* is available for those who desire a more in-depth study that can be used in combination or separately from these group guides.

In addition, you may want to keep the following list of suggestions in mind as you prepare to participate in your group discussions.[1]

1. The Contenders series does not require that the topics be discussed in an exact order. The guides, in addition to the topics within each guide, can be utilized in any order or even independently of each other, based on the needs of your group or class.

2. It is important to read over the material before each meeting (especially for leaders). The more familiar you are with the topic, the better your ability to discuss the issue during the actual group experience.

3. Actively participate in group discussion. The leader of this group is not expected to share a lecture, but to encourage each person to share in dialogue. This

includes both points of agreement and disagreement. Plan to share your beliefs openly and honestly.

4. Be sensitive to other people in the group. Listen attentively when others share and affirm whenever possible. It is important to show respect for the opinions of others even if they don't agree with your position. However, it is likewise important to affirm the biblical truths of each topic in wrapping up each area of discussion.

5. Be careful not to dominate the conversation. Feel free to share, but be sensitive to the length of time that you share in relation to the input of others in the group.

6. Stay focused on the discussion topic. Discussion can easily digress into side topics that may be equally important, but are unrelated to the session in discussion. As a leader, feel free to say: "That's a good issue to discuss. We should talk about that more sometime, but we need to get back to the topic for this session."

7. Encourage group participants to bring a Bible with them. While we believe there is no "perfect" Bible translation, we believe it is important to be sensitive to the needs of seekers and newer believers in your group by at least including a contemporary translation such as the New International Version or New Living Translation that can help provide quick understanding of Bible passages. Many good study Bibles with helpful notes are also available today to help group members in their growth. In these guides, the New International Version has been used unless otherwise noted.

8. Invest some extra time reading in the Bible, other recommended resources, or related audio and video content as you work through these sessions. The "Additional Resources" section at the back of each guide provides several such resources to enhance your growth.

The Greatest of These Is Love

Christianity is all about Christ. The very Son of God left the glory of heaven, was born of a woman, lived among ordinary people like you and me, and died a horrific death, before His resurrection and ascension back to heaven. Shortly before His death, He shared with His followers, "Greater love has no man than this, that he lay down his life for his friends" (John 15:13). Jesus provided a perfect example of this love by offering His life for us. As the apostle Paul later wrote, "Now these three remain: faith, hope, and love. But the greatest of these is love" (1 Corinthians 13:13).

As we learn to "contend for the faith," it is of utmost importance that we live with this same overwhelming love to those we encounter. The Christian faith provides more than ample evidence for the hope that we have in Christ. We invite you to explore these life-changing truths with others in a small-group context that leads to even further growth in your spiritual journey. May God bless you as you pursue the truth of Christ and "contend for the faith."

Setting the Stage: How Can God Allow Suffering and Evil?

9/11
The AIDS/HIV Epidemic
Hurricane Katrina
Cancer
War
Poverty

These and other issues often plague our minds with one probing question—*How can God allow suffering and evil?*

The problem of evil is one of the greatest challenges to the Christian faith made by skeptics today. Even for devoted followers of Christ, there is no greater test of faith than questions like, "If God really is all-powerful and loving, then why am I suffering this way?" "Why does a good God allow His children to suffer?" We see wars, hunger, violence, and natural disasters on television and question how God could really care about the predicament of those in need. Is God really there at all?

Some people blame fate or destiny, suggesting that evil has no rhyme or reason. Suffering is simply random. Others believe there is some evil force or spirits that wreak the havoc that causes today's problems. Many times, God Himself is blamed for catastrophes. In the insurance world, natural disasters are even called "acts of God."

Maybe you've heard a speaker mention that the problems we face in life are forms of testing, but does such a view cover every bad thing that happens in our lives? What about the miscarriage of a baby? How could that be considered a test from God? What about the loss of a parent, spouse, or child? Could God really be using such a tragedy to grow our faith?

These are tough questions, many of which the Bible tackles directly. In the Bible, "evil" is mentioned over 440 different times. God is familiar with the reality of evil and addresses it specifically. God is also intimately familiar with suffering. He addresses it 145 times in Scripture. One of the larger books of the Bible, the book of Job, is devoted primarily to this question. The books of Jeremiah and Habakkuk have much to say about it. About one third of the Psalms, the prayers of the Old Testament, are cries that arise out of doubt, disappointment, or pain. Even Jesus Christ experienced suffering and evil at the hands of others during his crucifixion.

Yet we still often feel that God doesn't seem to be there when the times are tough. Dr. Erwin Lutzer writes, "We must be careful about what we say about tragedies. If we say too much, we may err, thinking we can read the fine print of God's purposes. But if we say nothing, we give the impression that there is no message we can learn from calamities. I believe that God does speak through these events, but we must be cautious about thinking we know the details of his agenda."[2]

As we struggle with these difficult questions, take comfort that the Bible does provide reasonable answers for many of our longings. Let's begin the journey to discover what God's Word has to share on this vital issue of evil and suffering.

Where Did Suffering and Evil Begin?

Getting Started

We live in a fallen world. Terrorists blow themselves up in the name of Allah. The latest murder highlights the nightly news. Drug and alcohol abuse run rampant. Broken families have become more normal than traditional, two-parent families.

As we investigate the origins of suffering and evil, we must first admit that evil is real. We do not live in a perfect world. Christian leader Dr. Albert Mohler has written:

> Christianity does not deny the reality of evil or try to hide from its true horror. Christians dare not minimize evil nor take refuge in euphemisms. Beyond this, we cannot accept that evil will have the last word. The last word will be the perfect fulfillment of the grace and justice of God.[3]

Our culture is riddled with examples of the consequences of evil. When a husband has an affair, it damages his wife and children for a lifetime. A natural disaster such as Hurricane Katrina leaves its mark on communities and the entire nation for years into the future.

Another blemish on our culture is the issue of domestic abuse. Recent research indicates, for instance, that:

- Estimates range from nine hundred and sixty thousand incidents of violence against a current or former spouse, boyfriend, or girlfriend per year. One to three million women who are physically abused by their husband or boyfriend per year.
- Around the world, at least one in every three women has been beaten, coerced into sex, or otherwise abused during her lifetime.
- Nearly one-third of American women (31 percent) report being physically or sexually abused by a husband or boyfriend at some point in their lives, according to a 1998 Commonwealth Fund survey.
- Nearly twenty-five percent of American women report being raped and/or physically assaulted by a current or former spouse, cohabiting partner, or date at some time in their lifetime.
- Thirty percent of Americans say they know a woman who has been physically abused by her husband or boyfriend in the past year.[4]

Some people respond to such forms of evil by denying that a loving, caring God could co-exist with such problems. Either He is a poor creator or inept leader. In other words, God either created a messed-up world on purpose (a disturbing thought) or fails to have enough power to stop the problems in our world.

But is there any other option that makes sense? If there is a loving God in control of the universe, what explanation exists for the origin of evil—and its continuation—among people He created to live in relationship with Him?

Talk about It

1. What is something bad that has happened to you lately? What thoughts did you have about what God should have done in your situation?

   Had to take the ACT's, why did he let mom sign me up for them?! why am I so grumpy?

2. Who or what do we often blame for the problems we see in our lives and in the world around us? Why do you think we tend to place blame on these things or people? *Blame the people around us.*

   We don't want to take responsibility for our actions

Here's What I'm Thinking

Types of Evil

Philosophers and theologians have defined three primary categories of evil:

Moral Evil	Murder, rape, theft, lying, cheating
Natural Evil	Earthquakes, floods, hurricanes, human disease, famine
Combined	Human misuse of land causing a natural disaster like a mudslide; looting by humans that follows a major flood or hurricane

It's important to distinguish between these kinds of evil. Moral evil results from the actions of free creatures. Murder, rape, and theft are examples. Natural evil results from natural processes such as earthquakes and floods. Of course, sometimes the two are intermingled, such as when flooding results in loss of human life due to poor planning or shoddy construction of buildings. About these, pastor and author Dr. Erwin Lutzer writes:

> If natural disasters are out of God's control, then my life and my future are out of God's control. The weak God of modern liberalism is hardly able to speak comfort to those who seek it.[5]

3. Which category would some of the evils you mentioned in question one fall into—moral evil, natural evil, or a combination of the two? Does the type of evil influence who we tend to blame?

How Did Evil Enter Our World?

If God created everything (and Christians say He has), and since evil exists (and we believe it does exist), then isn't God the creator of evil? The answer is no.

Evil is real, but evil is not a thing. Evil is a lack of good things. For example, if you have a wound in your arm, the wound is not an additional thing; it is a lack of health and wholeness in your arm. If you rip the sleeve of your jacket, the tear is not something in addition to the jacket; it is a lack of wholeness for the jacket. Evil is a lack of what is good, similar to a bodily wound or tear in a garment. What exists is good, but the evil is the lack in the wholeness of what should be there.

4. If someone asked you why we live in a messed-up world that is full of evil, how would you respond?

   We live in a great world, where the evil is created by US.

How did evil enter our world? To answer this question, we must travel back to the Garden of Eden with Adam and Eve in Genesis 3. In verses 1-6, we find the progression of circumstances that led this couple from obedience to disobedience and the beginnings of evil.

> Now the serpent was more crafty than any
> of the wild animals the LORD God had made.
> He said to the woman, "Did God really
> say, 'You must not eat from any tree in the
> garden'?"

The woman said to the serpent, "We may eat
fruit from the trees in the garden, but God
did say, 'You must not eat fruit from the tree
that is in the middle of the garden, and you
must not touch it, or you will die.'"

"You will not surely die," the serpent said to
the woman. "For God knows that when you
eat of it your eyes will be opened, and you
will be like God, knowing good and evil."

When the woman saw that the fruit of the tree
was good for food and pleasing to the eye,
and also desirable for gaining wisdom, she
took some and ate it. She also gave some to
her husband, who was with her, and he ate it.

Eve did four things that marked this entry of sin into the
human race:

- *Temptation:*   She *saw* that the fruit looked good.
- *Initiation:*   She *took* the fruit.
- *Execution:*   She *ate* the fruit.
- *Extension:*   She *gave* the fruit to Adam to eat.

5. From your reading of the verses above, does the
    biblical account of sin and evil entering the world
    suggest that God created sin? Why or why not?

no, b/c god said it was bad.

6. If God did not create sin as part of His original creation, what option makes the most sense for evil's origin:

- God did not expect evil to enter the world and is unable to stop it.
- God must not really exist after all.
- God allowed for sin without directly creating it. He created humans with the ability to choose good and evil.

"Your eyes are too pure to look on evil; you cannot tolerate wrong. Why then do you tolerate the treacherous? Why are you silent while the wicked swallow up those more righteous than themselves?" —Habakkuk 1:13

Notice in this last option that God created the *fact* of freedom, while humans perform the *acts* of freedom. God made evil *possible*, but His created beings made evil *a reality*. The ability to do something does not necessitate doing it. God is able to control everything, yet He allows free will.

The Role of Human Choice

In an interview I (John) conducted with theologian and professor Dr. Norman Geisler, I asked him how he answers the question, "Where did the evil come from that is in this world?"

His response was:

> According to the Bible, God is absolutely good and he made an absolutely good world. Everything he made, he said it is good. Every creature of God is good.

One of the good things that he gave some of those good creatures was free will. It is good to be free. Hardly anyone would say freedom is bad . . . [but] freedom is the source of evil, because if you are really free to love God, you are also free not to love him. . . . So evil arose from free will. Freedom is a good. God created the good of freedom. Man performs the acts of evil by misusing his freedom.

7. According to the above quote, free choice resulted in the opportunity for evil to enter the world. With such great risk involved, why would a loving God give people the opportunity to do evil?

It is the peoples choice, God did not give them evil, they misused their freedom

Why Do Natural Disasters Occur?

It is important to realize we live in a fallen world as a result of our first ancestors, Adam and Eve, who chose to disobey God. This brought negative consequences, including:

1. A broken relationship with God (Genesis 3:22–24).
2. A curse on the natural world (Genesis 3:17–19).
3. Increased pains in childbearing (Genesis 3:16).

As a result, even though we are free creatures, we live in a world affected by the wrong use of human choice. Further, we live in a world in which consistent natural processes allow us to predict with some certainty the outcome of our choices and actions.

We can notice something striking about the natural laws God has instituted. Gravity is a natural process without which we could not function. Yet if we fall out of a tree, or step off of a roof, this same good natural law could result in great harm.

While some cataclysmic events in nature may be direct, causal "acts of God," others may be necessary byproducts of the creation of a world suitable for life. Plate tectonics, while resulting in earthquakes, tsunamis, and volcanoes for instance, also play a role in the development of petroleum deposits.

"Do not those who plot evil go astray? But those who plan what is good find love and faithfulness." —Proverbs 14:22

The water cycle brings flash floods, hurricanes, mudslides, and tornadoes, but also distributes water to crops and cattle. In other words, sometimes evil is a byproduct of a good thing. It is good to have water to drink, to irrigate crops, or to use for swimming or fishing. But a by-product of that good is that we could also drown in the same water. The assumption that God could have created a world free of natural catastrophes if truly benevolent requires a level of total knowledge that only God holds.

It is not only unnecessary, but also impossible, to completely understand why natural disasters occur and destroy property, animals, and human lives. It is important to understand that though we know God controls nature, sometimes God allows things to happen for reasons our finite minds cannot explain. Though we have God's Word to guide us, we do not have the answers to all of life's big questions, including the mysterious ways of our Creator. To connect particular natural disasters to the actions or problems of a particular group of people is speculation that only compounds already difficult situations.

8. Why is it important not to speculate that a natural disaster is God's judgment on a group of people or city?

God created nature, and nature took its course

9. How is Job's response in Job 1:18–22 an example for how we can respond to disasters in our lives?

It is not God and we cannot blame him.

What Now?

10. If you could trade your own free will in exchange for the elimination of evil and suffering, would you? Why or why not?

Honestly. depends

11. Name a recent natural disaster that has occurred. What are some of the difficult parts to accept from this tragedy? What are some possible positive results that have emerged from this tragedy?

Hurricane Iven.
Gas prices!!

12. Why do you think people become angry at God for bad things that happen in life?

Afraid to take responsibility

Consider This

This session is the start of an investigation into the problem of evil and suffering from a Christian perspective. You are not expected to start with all of the right answers. The only expectation is to have an open viewpoint and a desire to learn. In fact, you are probably involved in this group right now due to your curiosity to discover answers regarding some of your own doubts, or at least the doubts of others in your life. Rather than pretending to have the issues all figured out, feel free to express some of your difficult questions and concerns as you continue with this group. The only way to find the answers to your questions is to ask the real questions that still exist in your own mind.

To help identify ways your viewpoints or beliefs are growing during these sessions, throughout this series you will have moments to express where you currently stand on this journey. As you continue to learn, you may find some of your opinions changing from one session to the next. The key idea to remember is that this is a time of growth rather than a test. The more time you invest seeking the truth, the better your understanding will become on the issues discussed in this study guide.

13. Which of the following statements best describes your personal perspective on the issue of suffering of evil? (Circle all that apply.)

   A. Evil is an illusion and does not exist.
   B. Evil proves that God does not exist.
   C. Evil and good are relative terms and impossible to objectively define.
   D. Our freedom of choice has nothing to do with God.
   E. Our freedom of choice is a gift from God.
   F. God allows for evil, but does not desire it.
   G. Other thoughts:

Why Doesn't God Do Something about Suffering and Evil?

Getting Started

You're driving down the expressway when a fast-moving red sports car cuts you off like he's fighting for the pole position at the Indy 500. You slam on your brakes, nearly destroying your own vehicle in the process. In the end, you have a lapful of coffee and a flipped over purse on your floorboard.

Your boss promotes your coworker over you, despite the fact that he is continually late to the office, shops for his next car online when he should be working, and offers plenty of gossip to stir up controversies around the workplace. You, on the other hand, have put in long hours, focused on doing your job right, and do your best to encourage those around you rather than spread rumors.

This year, you plan on the perfect Christmas holiday with your family . . . until Uncle Mike shows up completely wasted. It isn't the first time, but this year was supposed to be different. Why did he have to ruin the special occasion for everyone?

You've probably experienced something similar to at least one of the above scenarios. When life doesn't seem fair, how does it make us feel? Angry? Discouraged? Disappointed? Often, we think God should have done something to change the situation. When He doesn't, it can naturally cause us to doubt who He really is and possibly whether He is even there at all.

These feelings pull at our hearts even more deeply when the issues transition from everyday problems to life-altering tragedies. When a parent loses a young child, why doesn't God do something about it? When a friend or loved one is afflicted with cancer, we wonder why this disease has afflicted a person we care about? When our own personal health comes under attack, we certainly have second thoughts about life. Late at night, when we are staring at the ceiling because of an injustice from earlier in the day, there are many times a common question emerges from deep within the recesses of our soul—Why doesn't God do something about it?

One writer has even claimed, "There is a fundamental sense in which evil is not something that can be made sense of. The essence of evil is that it is something which is absurd, bizarre and irrational. It is the nature of evil to be inexplicable, an enigma and a stupidity."[6]

Is God really there? And if He is, does He care about what is happening in our daily lives or not? If He is really all-powerful and loving, why couldn't He end the AIDS crisis, stop a tsunami or hurricane from devastating lives, or heal our loved ones when they are sick? Couldn't He at least cause that sports car that cuts us off to have a flat tire?

Why doesn't God do something about suffering and evil?

Talk about It

1. When is a time you wished that you could have changed a difficult situation that had occurred? What did the situation cause you to wonder about God's role in your life?

2. What are some of the common thoughts people have about God during difficult times?

3. If God could stop evil and suffering, why doesn't He?

Here's What I'm Thinking

The Persistence of Evil

Another aspect of the problem of evil is its persistence. *Why* does God allow it? Even if He did not produce it, He does permit it. Yet He is also supposed to be all-powerful and could destroy it. So why doesn't He?

According to philosopher-theologian Dr. Norman Geisler, the classical way to state the *problem* of the persistence of evil is as follows:[7]

1. If God is all good, he *would* destroy evil.
2. If God is all powerful, he *could* destroy evil.
3. But evil is not destroyed.
4. Therefore, there is no such God.

Put this way, the argument leaves open the possibility of God, but not God as defined in the Bible. Every finite or limited being has a cause. So a finite god is only a creature that needs an infinite Creator. (In other words, a god who is not all-powerful requires an infinite, all-powerful God to create it.) And since God is powerful, then He must be infinitely powerful. Likewise, since He is good, He must be infinitely good.

"The fact of suffering undoubtedly constitutes the single greatest challenge to the Christian faith. . . . Sensitive spirits ask if it can possibly be reconciled with God's justice and love."
—John Stott[8]

So, a finite god is not an option for a person who believes in the existence of God. God has both the desire *and ability* needed to do anything possible. But He is not going to destroy our freedom to deal with evil. He will ultimately defeat it.

The proper perspective we must have on this issue is one that separates evil in our world today from how God will ultimately deal with evil in the future. The outline of this view is:

1. God is all good and *desires* to defeat evil.
2. God is all powerful and is *able* to defeat evil.
3. Evil is not yet defeated.
4. Therefore, it will *one day* be defeated.

Notice, the atheist says, "Evil is not defeated, and never will be. Therefore, there is no God." But how could anyone know that evil will never be defeated unless he were God? It would be like reading one sentence randomly from a book, throwing the book away, and then saying, "This could never turn out right."

For those who follow Christ, there is the conviction that God is not only all-powerful, but can and will eventually eliminate all suffering and evil from the world. Evil may exist today, but it will not exist forever.

The Old Testament prophet Habakkuk expressed similar thoughts long ago:

How long, O LORD, must I call for help,
    but you do not listen?
    Or cry out to you, "Violence!"
    but you do not save?
Why do you make me look at injustice?
    Why do you tolerate wrong?
    Destruction and violence are before me;
    there is strife, and conflict abounds. (Habakkuk 1:2–3)

However, God's response to Habakkuk, that he would bring future judgment on the nations invading Israel, helped him put his concerns in their proper perspective. Evil and suffering exist in this life, but will not last forever. In the end, Habakkuk could sing:

Though the fig tree does not bud
    and there are no grapes on the vines,
    though the olive crop fails
    and the fields produce no food,
    though there are no sheep in the pen
    and no cattle in the stalls,
    yet I will rejoice in the LORD,
    I will be joyful in God my Savior. (Habakkuk 3:17–18)

According to Habakkuk, there was ultimately no inconsistency between the existence of evil and a loving God, as God will someday defeat all evil and straighten out all injustices.

In Psalm 96:13, the songwriter also penned, "They will sing before the LORD, for he comes, he comes to judge the earth. He will judge the world in righteousness and the peoples in his truth." Here, the Bible rejoices also in the promise that God will at last end all evil and suffering through His perfect final judgment.

4. Have you ever shared the same questions about God that Habakkuk expressed above? What was the cause of your questioning? How was your long-term response similar to Habakkuk's viewpoint in 3:17–18? How was it different?

5. If someone asked you, "How can you believe in God when there is so much evil in the world?" how could you respond? How is it logically possible to believe in both the existence of God and evil?

6. Habakkuk asked God tough questions in his book. How do you think God feels about us asking Him the deep, questioning thoughts of our hearts?

Evil and Suffering Strengthen the Fact that God Exists

Did you realize that the existence of evil and suffering can actually help show that God does exist? If we say evil does not exist, then we are assuming there is no absolute standard of good. If there were no absolute standard of good, we could not claim to know anything was evil. In order for an absolute good to exist, God is necessary.

We must have someone who draws a straight line that will serve as the standard for declaring another line crooked. Only an absolutely righteous Being can draw a line of absolute good. There cannot be an ultimate moral standard of good without an ultimate Lawgiver, and that lawgiver is God.

Charlie Campbell shares the following five-step reasoning:

1. Evil exists in the world.
2. Evil is a departure from the way things should be.
3. If there is a way things should be, there must be a standard or design to the universe.
4. There cannot be a design without a designer of the universe.
5. Evil is ultimately humanity's departure from the standard and design provided by the intelligent designer, God.

Here's how it might go in a conversation:

> "So, we can agree that evil does exist in the world?"

> Yes."

> "Would you agree that evil is a departure from the way things *ought* to be?"

> "Hmmm. I'm not sure. . . ."

> "You yourself have looked at the world and

have seen the famines and the diseases, and the wars, and have thought this is not the way things *ought* to be. They should be better. So then, evil is simply a departure (or deviation) from the way things *ought* to be. Can we agree with that?"

"Yes."

"If there is a way things *ought* to be, there must be a designed plan (or designed standard) for the universe. So it would logically follow, and correct me if I'm wrong, that there cannot be a way that the universe ought to be (a designed plan for the universe) without a designer of the universe.

"Why's that?" or "I disagree."

"But you cannot have a plan, or a way the universe *ought* to be if the universe is just the result of some random explosion, or accident. If the universe came into existence from nothing and by nothing (which seems foolish, but that is what atheists believe) then there cannot exist a way things are supposed to be. The universe *should* experience suffering, diseases, death, and we could never say that anything is wrong about those things.[9]

7. How convinced are you about the suggestion that evil and suffering offer evidence for God's existence?

8. Some people will actually suggest that evil does not really exist but is merely an illusion (as is taught in Hinduism). How does such a suggestion strike you? Do you think it makes more sense to believe in evil as an illusion or as a real occurrence? If evil is real, then how does this point people toward the reality of a creator God who offers a better life than we experience in this world?

SESSION 2

The End of Evil

If the Bible merely confirmed that evil and suffering existed without offering an alternative or some kind of solution, we would still be left without hope. However, God has communicated that there is a point at which evil will ultimately be defeated. Those who trust in Jesus Christ will spend eternity with God in an environment without evil:

> *"He will wipe every tear from their eyes.*
> *There will be no more death or mourning or*
> *crying or pain, for the old order of things has*
> *passed away."*
>
> *He who was seated on the throne said,*
> *"I am making everything new!" Then he*
> *said, "Write this down, for these words are*
> *trustworthy and true."* (Revelation 21:4–5)

It is inaccurate to claim that evil has always existed and will always exist. According to God's Word, evil began when God's created beings chose to disobey His plan. Even so, God has a plan for the complete removal of evil as part of His ultimate redemption of His people.

9. How does believing that evil will one day end help change our perspective regarding evil and suffering in the world today?

"The question should not be, 'Will God stop evil?' but, 'When will He stop evil?' "
—Ken Boa and Larry Moody, *I'm Glad You Asked*[10]

---

10. In what ways can we encourage those who are in difficult situations and perhaps help them with their current problems? How do the words of Romans 12:15 help provide a balanced response?

11. Why do you think so many people today automatically deny that Jesus performed miracles?

What Now?

12. What resources does God provide to help in our struggles with evil and suffering? What is one specific way you could encourage someone currently struggling with a problem?

13. In what ways can we respond during difficult situations that both help those in need and communicate the truth of God's ultimate power over evil? How do Christians often misrepresent God when answering questions pertaining to why suffering occurs? How could we offer a more helpful response?

14. Since many people outside of Christianity have questions about suffering in our world, what are some ways you could use this issue to talk about who God is and point a person toward a relationship with Christ?

Consider This

On a scale of one to five, what response best describes your personal beliefs regarding the following statements about evil and suffering?

15. Evil is not real; it is simply an illusion:

1	2	3	4	5
Don't believe	Believe somewhat	Some of it is true	Mostly true	Completely accurate

16. Evil and suffering make it difficult to believe in an all-powerful God:

1	2	3	4	5
Don't believe	Believe somewhat	Some of it is true	Mostly true	Completely accurate

17. The existence of evil and suffering actually offer significant evidence for the existence of God:

1	2	3	4	5
Don't believe	Believe somewhat	Some of it is true	Mostly true	Completely accurate

18. The biblical view of evil's existence and ultimate end makes the most sense to me:

1	2	3	4	5
Don't believe	Believe somewhat	Some of it is true	Mostly true	Completely accurate

19 What questions still remain for you regarding why God does not stop evil in the world?

Why Do Good Things Happen to Bad People, and Bad Things to Good People?

Getting Started

Philip Yancey, in his book *Disappointment with God*, provocatively addresses the question of why life appears unfair:

> Some Jewish writers, such as Jerzy Kosinski and Elie Wiesel, began with a strong faith in God, but saw it vaporize in the gas furnaces of the Holocaust. Face to face with history's grossest unfairness, they concluded that God must not exist. (Still, the human instinct asserts itself. Kosinski and Wiesel overlook the underlying issue of where our primal sense of fairness comes from. Why ought we even expect the world to be fair?) Others, equally mindful of the world's unfairness, cannot bring themselves to deny God's

existence. Instead, they propose another possibility: perhaps God agrees that life is unfair, but cannot do anything about it.

Rabbi Harold Kushner took this approach in his best-selling book *When Bad Things Happen to Good People*. After watching his son die of the disease progeria, Kushner concluded that "even God has a hard time keeping chaos in check," and that God is "a God of justice and not of power."

According to Rabbi Kushner, God is as frustrated, even outraged, by the unfairness on this planet as anyone else, but he lacks the power to change it. Millions of readers found comfort in Kushner's portrayal of a God who seemed compassionate, albeit weak. I wonder, however, what those people make of the last five chapters of Job, which contain God's "self-defense." No other part of the Bible conveys God's power so impressively. If God is less-than-powerful, why did he choose the worst possible situation, when his power was most called into question, to insist on his omnipotence? (Elie Wiesel said of the God described by Kushner, "If that's who God is, why doesn't he resign and let someone more competent take his place?").[11]

When life goes wrong, either for ourselves or someone else we know, it is only natural to question why it is happening. We sometimes wonder, how God can allow innocent children to suffer from life-ending diseases? Why do people continue to be mistreated based on the money they make, the home they live in, the clothing they wear, or the color of their skin?

Even skeptics or those outside of any faith system desire for the wrongs of this world to be changed. There is something deep within our hearts that longs for the injustices of this life to be corrected.

How can God allow bad things to happen to good people and good things to happen to bad people? It seems like a fair question to ask. If God is just, why isn't life?

Talk about It

1. Mention a time you or someone you know seemed to suffer an injustice for no reason. How did it make you feel?

2. Why do you think people tend to blame God when life goes wrong or innocent people suffer?

3. Describe a time you caused or contributed to the suffering you experienced. Did you still have a desire to blame someone else? Why or why not?

SESSION 3

Here's What I'm Thinking

What Good Can Come from Suffering?

Found in the clothing of a dead child at Ravensbruck concentration camp was the following prayer:

> *O Lord, remember not only the men and women of good will, but also those of ill will. But do not remember all of the suffering they have inflicted upon us:*
>
> *Instead remember the fruits we have borne because of this suffering, our fellowship, our loyalty to one another, our humility, our courage, our generosity, the greatness of heart that has grown from this trouble.*
>
> *When our persecutors come to be judged by you, let all of these fruits that we have borne be their forgiveness.* (source unknown)

Suffering is not usually an enjoyable experience. However, good can be found even during times of suffering, even in the most extreme situations. In our book *Defending Your Faith* (AMG Publishers), we share the following reasons as to why people sometimes suffer:

- As an example to others
- To better sympathize with others
- To remain humble
- As a learning tool
- To depend on God's power
- To grow in our relationship with Christ (developing the fruit of the Spirit—Galatians 5:2–23)
- To reveal the need for God's discipline in our lives
- To further the work of Christ (such as when the mistreatment of a missionary opens up opportunities

to impact others with Christ's love)

A great biblical example can be found in Philippians 1:12–14, where we read:

> Now I want you to know, brothers, that
> what has happened to me has really served to
> advance the gospel. As a result, it has become
> clear throughout the whole palace guard
> and to everyone else that I am in chains for
> Christ. Because of my chains, most of the
> brothers in the Lord have been encouraged
> to speak the word of God more courageously
> and fearlessly.

In this situation, Paul had been arrested for telling people that Jesus had come back to life. During his time under house arrest, he had the opportunity to share with all of the guards and those who visited him about the reason he had been arrested. As a result, the Christian faith spread to new people and encouraged other believers to speak out with boldness.

4. When is a time you have seen a difficult situation in your life lead to a positive result in the future?

5. Which of the above reasons for suffering is the most difficult to understand or accept? Which reasons have you been able to see at work in your own life?

6. How did Paul's response to his time of suffering influence the impact of his life? How can our attitude toward suffering help or hurt the outcome of the difficulties we face?

Where Is God When We Suffer?

Over sixty years ago, Elie Wiesel was a fifteen-year old prisoner in the Nazi work camp at Buna, a sub-camp of the infamous Auschwitz-Birkenau concentration camp complex. A cache of arms belonging to a Dutchman was discovered at the camp. The man was promptly shipped to the extermination camp area of Auschwitz. But he had a young servant boy, a *pipel* as they were called, a child with a refined and beautiful face, unheard of in the camps. He had the face of a sad angel. The little servant, like his Dutch master, was cruelly tortured, but would not reveal any information. So the SS sentenced the child to death, along with two other prisoners who had been discovered with arms. Wiesel tells the story:

> One day when we came back from work,
> we saw three gallows rearing up in the
> assembly place, three black crows. Roll call.
> SS all around us; machine guns trained:
> the traditional ceremony. Three victims in
> chains—and one of them, the little servant,
> the sad-eyed angel. The SS seemed more
> preoccupied, more disturbed than usual. To
> hang a young boy in front of thousands of
> spectators was no light matter. The head of
> the camp read the verdict. All eyes were on

the child. He was lividly pale, almost calm, biting his lips. The gallows threw its shadow over him. This time the Lagercapo refused to act as executioner. Three SS replaced him. The three victims mounted together onto the chairs. The three necks were placed at the same moment within the nooses. "Long live liberty!" cried the two adults. But the child was silent.

"Where is God? Where is He?" someone behind me asked. Total silence throughout the camp. On the horizon, the sun was setting. "Bare your heads!" yelled the head of the camp. His voice was raucous. We were weeping. "Cover your heads!" Then the march past began. The two adults were no longer alive. Their tongues hung swollen, blue-tinged. But the third rope was still moving; being so light, the child was still alive. . . . For more than half an hour he stayed there, struggling between life and death, dying in slow agony under our eyes. And we had to look him full in the face. He was still alive when I passed in front of him. His tongue was still red, his eyes were not yet glazed. Behind me, I heard the same man asking: "Where is God now?" And I heard a voice within me answer him: "Where is He? Here He is—He is hanging here on this gallows."[12]

Despite the pain of Elie Weisel's experience, the response is right on target. God is there with us when we suffer, and promises to correct all wrongs at His judgment. How do we know this for certain? It is because His ultimate expression of this truth can be found in the fact that Jesus, the only Son of God, offered His life to the suffering he experienced on a Roman cross to make it possible for us to have our broken relationship with God restored, and to provide the gift of eternal life to those who will receive it. Betrayed by a close friend and abandoned by His followers, Jesus felt the emotions and the physical pain that we experience during our times of suffering. As a result, He is able to identify with us when we suffer in our daily struggles.

As the book of Hebrews observes,

> Therefore, since we have a great high priest who has gone through the heavens, Jesus the Son of God, let us hold firmly to the faith we profess. For *we do not have a high priest who is unable to sympathize with our weaknesses, but we have one who has been tempted in every way, just as we are—yet was without sin.* Let us then approach the throne of grace with confidence, so that we may receive mercy and find grace to help us in our time of need. (Hebrews 4:14–16, emphasis added)

7. Why does God seem far away when we suffer? How does it make you feel to know that He is with us even during our most difficult moments?

8. How is suffering a different experience for a person who does not have a personal relationship with God? In what ways does suffering cause people to seek for the hope that only Christ provides?

9. Is the statement from Hebrews that Jesus is able to identify with our struggles helpful in understanding God's presence during our suffering? Why or why not?

"God whispers to us in our pleasures, speaks in our conscience, but shouts in our pain; it is His megaphone to rouse a deaf world."
—C.S. Lewis, The Problem of Pain[13]

The God of Comfort

Skeptics argue that God, if He exists, cannot be loving since He allows suffering and evil. However, the Bible presents God as loving despite the pain we often endure in this life. A few examples include:

And we know that in all things God works for the good of those who love him, who have been called according to his purpose.
(Romans 8:28)

Who shall separate us from the love of Christ? Shall trouble or hardship or persecution or famine or nakedness or danger or sword? . . . No, in all these things we are more than conquerors through him who loved us. For I am convinced that neither death nor life, neither angels nor demons,

*neither the present nor the future, nor
any powers, neither height nor depth, nor
anything else in all creation, will be able to
separate us from the love of God that is in
Christ Jesus our Lord.* (Romans 8:35, 37–39)

*For God did not appoint us to suffer wrath
but to receive salvation through our Lord
Jesus Christ.* (1 Thessalonians 5:9)

*Dear friends, do not be surprised at the
painful trial you are suffering, as though
something strange were happening to you.
But rejoice that you participate in the
sufferings of Christ, so that you may be
overjoyed when his glory is revealed. If you
are insulted because of the name of Christ,
you are blessed, for the Spirit of glory and
of God rests on you. If you suffer, it should
not be as a murderer or thief or any other
kind of criminal, or even as a meddler.
However, if you suffer as a Christian, do not
be ashamed, but praise God that you bear
that name. . . . Those who suffer according to
God's will should commit themselves to their
faithful Creator and continue to do good.*
(1 Peter 4:12–16, 19)

As evangelist Billy Graham has written, "Nowhere does the
Bible teach that Christians are exempt from the tribulations
and natural disasters that come upon the world. Scripture does
teach that the Christian can face tribulation, crisis, calamity,
and personal suffering with a supernatural power that is not
available to the person outside of Christ."[14]

10. What do the verses above say about the response
those who follow Christ should have regarding

suffering? How have you seen this applied well in the life of someone you know?

11. Why does the Bible teach that those who suffer for their faith should praise God? What do you think would happen if more people applied this verse to their lives today?

What Now?

12. What is an area in your life in which you are currently experiencing a struggle? How could the information shared in this session apply to your situation?

13. In addition to your personal struggles, the Bible challenges us to help others in their time of difficulty. Who is someone you could help now who is going through a difficult time?

14. Which of this session's verses stood out to you the most? Consider writing it on a note card or typing it into your cell phone to carry with you to read and memorize over the next week.

Consider This

Read the following statements and circle the response that best describes your opinion:

15. The Bible's view of suffering . . .
    A. makes the most sense to me.
    B. answers some of my questions about suffering, but I still have a lot of unanswered questions.
    C. hasn't been very helpful for my spiritual journey.
    D. I'm not sure what I believe about it.
    E. OTHER: _____

16. The reasons people suffer . . .
    A. always have a clear explanation.
    B. can sometimes be understood, but not always.
    C. are completely beyond human understanding.
    D. I'm not sure what I believe about it.
    E. OTHER: _____

17. Suffering as a follower of Christ . . .
    A. is much different since Christians have God's Spirit to assist them.
    B. doesn't make much of a difference. Suffering is still tough.
    C. I'm not sure what I think about suffering.
    D. OTHER: _____

SESSION 3

Do Heaven and Hell Really Exist?

Getting Started

How can Christians claim to be so certain there is a heaven and hell beyond this life? Is there some kind of solid evidence? What about reincarnation? If we're just speculating on what's on the other side, why does it matter what we believe? It seems like some people just make up heaven because that's where they want to go.

Even if heaven does exist, how can a person be sure it is the place to be? If it's really a place where people wear white robes and play harps all day, what's the point? Angels may make for good television, but what kind of eternal bliss can be found through boredom?

Of course, the flip side, hell, doesn't sound like much fun either. If it's all about burning forever with a red guy with pointy horns and a pitchfork, why can't we just rot in the ground when this life is through? Maybe when life is over, it's just over. And even if something *is* there, whom can we trust to provide accurate information about the afterlife?

Should we really listen to all of those books or speakers who talk about their near-death and afterlife experiences? Who's to say they aren't making it up or didn't just have some kind of elaborate dream?

People point toward the future as if heaven makes up for all of the lame things that happen during our lives on earth. Isn't that just wishful thinking? Will those who believe in Jesus really have it made in heaven while everyone else suffers for eternity? That doesn't sound fun or fair. In some ways, aren't all of these faith issues similar to stories about the Easter bunny or Mother Goose—stories that sound great but fail to portray reality?

When we get to the bottom line, how do we know there is a heaven or a hell or if other options might exist? What does the Bible say about what happens in the next life?

In this session, we'll explore what God's Word says about the afterlife, including heaven and hell, and why these eternal destinations are important to the issue of suffering and evil in our lives today.

We'll discover that though these issues are based on faith, they are not unreasonable. Even more importantly, our eternal destination is based on choices made in this life. If there are no reruns or no reincarnation, then this life is the only chance we get. And if there is something beyond this life that extends past the grave, wouldn't it be important to know as much as we can about it?

Talk about It

1. Do you believe there is some kind of afterlife? On what is your belief based?

2. Several options have been suggested regarding what happens to us upon physical death. In which of the following options do you believe? Do any of these views seem to contradict one another? What helped you choose your view on this issue?

Annihilation	Reincarnation	Purgatory	Universalism	Works-based Afterlife	Biblical Christianity
Life ends at physical death	Life repeats in various forms	An afterlife "middle ground" between heaven and hell where many stay before going to heaven	Everyone spends afterlife in heaven	Afterlife will be determined by how many good deeds a person has done	Those who know Jesus by faith go to heaven; those who do not go to hell. Rejects the other five views

3. What are some of your questions about what happens to people after death?

Here's What I'm Thinking

God Claims that Human Life Is Eternal

The Bible repeatedly claims that this life is not all that there is. John's Gospel, written specifically to help people come to faith in Jesus Christ, shares numerous examples:[15]

1	*... that everyone who believes in him may have **eternal life**.*	3:5
2	*... whoever believes in him shall not perish but have **eternal life**.*	3:16
3	*Whoever believes in the Son has **eternal life** ...*	3:36
4	*... the water I give him will become in him a spring of water welling up to **eternal life**.*	4:14
5	*... even now he harvests the crop for **eternal life**.*	4:36

SESSION 4

6	You diligently study the Scriptures because you think that by them you possess **eternal life**. These are the Scriptures that testify about me, yet you refuse to come to me to have life.	5:38–39
7	Do not work for food that spoils, but for food that endures to **eternal life**, which the Son of Man will give you.	6:27
8	Everyone who looks to the Son and believes in him shall have **eternal life.**	6:40
9	Whoever eats my flesh and drinks my blood has **eternal life**, and I will raise him up at the last day.	6:54
10	Lord, to whom shall we go? You have the words of **eternal life**.	6:68
11	I give them **eternal life**, and they shall never perish . . .	10:28
12	The man who loves his life will lose it, while the man who hates his life in this world will keep it for **eternal life**.	12:25
13	For I did not speak of my own accord, but the Father who sent me commanded me what to say and how to say it. I know that his command leads to **eternal life**.	12:49–50
14	For you granted him authority over all people that he might give **eternal life** to all those you have given him.	17:2

4. On a scale of one to ten, how confident are you about your afterlife? What unresolved questions do you need answered for your confidence to increase?

5. According to these verses from John's Gospel, how does a person obtain eternal life with God in heaven?

All about Heaven

The apostle John describes heaven by sharing the following words of Jesus:

> In my Father's house are many rooms; if it
> were not so, I would have told you. I am
> going there to prepare a place for you. And if
> I go and prepare a place for you, I will come
> back and take you to be with me that you
> also may be where I am. (John 14:2–3)

Here, we are told heaven includes many rooms, that Jesus would go there to personally prepare a place for those who would one day live there, and that He would return to take His followers there with Him.

Heaven will be a perfect environment. There will be no need to worry about someone breaking into our home. There will be no washing dishes, taking out the trash, doing laundry, or mowing the lawn. Heaven will be a perfect place, with no need for home improvement. While our current world is filled

SESSION 4

with much evil and physical decay, our new home in heaven will be one of perfection. The Bible tells us heaven will be a place...

- where Jesus is (Philippians 1:23).
- a place of perfection beyond our comprehension (1 Corinthians 2:9).
- called paradise (Revelation 2:7).
- without tears, death, sadness, or pain (Revelation 21:4).
- where all who have believed in Christ will live together for eternity (Revelation 21:27).
- where everything will be new (Revelation 21:5).
- with no sin or anything wrong (Revelation 22:3).

6. How does the way Jesus and John describe heaven appeal to you? How does this view differ from our cultural views about heaven?

7. Do you think we should be concerned about people who claim to have visions of heaven during near-death experiences? How can we determine if their stories are genuine or not, or is it even possible to do so?

All about Hell

Hell is not a popular place. According to a Barna Group survey, seventy-one percent of Americans believe that hell exists, but only *one-half of one percent expect to go to hell* upon their death. Nearly two-thirds of Americans (64%) believe they will go to heaven. One in twenty adults (5%) claim they will come back as another life form, while the same proportion (5%) contend they will simply cease to exist.[16]

---

*"Few people take hell seriously, but it is very real,
and it is worse than we could ever imagine."*
—David L. Hocking[17]

But what does the Bible claim on this important topic? There are a variety of terms used to describe hell. The original Old Testament word frequently used for the grave is *Sheol* (used in older English translations as well). Sometimes it simply refers to the grave (Psalm 49:15). Other times it is described as a place of dread (Psalm 30:9), sorrow (Isaiah 38:3), or punishment (Job 24:19).

Biblical Terms Referring to Hell		
Hades	The dwelling place of the wicked dead	Used 11 times in New Testament
Tartaros	Home of wicked angels	Jude 6–7
Lake of Fire	The second death	Revelation 20:15 (5 times in Revelation)

SESSION 4

Biblical Terms Referring to Hell		
Bottomless Pit (some translations "the Abyss")	The lower regions as the home of demons	Revelation 9:1 (used 6 times in Revelation)
Gehenna	Place where children were sacrificed to Molech in fire	Jeremiah 7:31; Matthew 23:33
Outer Darkness	Place where there is weeping and gnashing of teeth	Matthew 8:12; 22:13; 25:30
Place of Torment	Used in same context as Hades	Luke 16:28
Fiery Furnace	Place angels will throw evildoers	Matthew 13:42
Everlasting Destruction	Place those who do not know God will be sent	2 Thessalonians 1:8–9
Eternal Punishment	Place Jesus says the wicked will go	Matthew 25:46
Exclusion from God's Presence	The result of each of the above	John 16:11

Hell is also described in detail in various places throughout the Bible. Specifically, hell is described as a place of...

- Everlasting punishment: Matthew 25:46.
- Eternal condemnation: Mark 3:29.
- Eternal judgment: Hebrews 6:2.
- Everlasting destruction: 2 Thessalonians 1:9.

- Eternal fire: Matthew 18:8–9 (*Gehenna*); Matthew 25:41; Jude 7.
- Unquenchable fire: Mark 9:43–48 (see also Isaiah 66:24).
- Eternal torment: Revelation 19:20; 20:10.[18]

Chuck Colson, president of Prison Fellowship, writes:

> In a sense, the concept of hell gives meaning to our lives. It tells us that the moral choices we make day by day have eternal significance, that our behavior has consequences lasting to eternity, that God Himself takes our choices seriously.
>
> The doctrine of hell is not just some dusty theological holdover from the Middle Ages. It has significant social consequences. Without a conviction of ultimate justice, people's sense of moral obligation dissolves, and social bonds are broken.
>
> Of course, these considerations are not the most important reason to believe in hell. Jesus repeatedly issued warnings that if we turn away from God in this life, we will be alienated from God eternally.
>
> And yet, although "the wages of sin is death," Paul also says that "the gift of God is eternal life in Christ Jesus our Lord" (Romans 6:23). While breath remains, it is never too late to turn to God in repentance, and when we ask for forgiveness, God eagerly grants it.
>
> (from *Answers to Your Kids' Questions*, Chuck Colson, 2000 Prison Fellowship Ministries.)

SESSION 4

8. Jesus spoke plainly about the reality and suffering of hell. In fact, He talked about hell more than anyone else. How does Jesus describe hell in Matthew 10:27–30? How does this description fit your previous view of hell?

What about Other Options?

Does the Bible ever hint at other afterlife options, such as purgatory or reincarnation? Not really. Luke 16:19–31 indicates that unbelievers go to a place of suffering upon death, not into another body. This is why the apostle Paul emphasized that "now is the day of salvation" (2 Corinthians 6:2).

"Hell is one of the chief grounds on which Christianity is attacked as barbarous and the goodness of God impugned."
—C. S. Lewis, *The Problem of Pain*[19]

The clearest expression of what happens at death is found in Jesus' account of Lazarus and the rich man in Luke 16:20–31. It clearly states that Lazarus was taken to Abraham's side (a phrase that referred to being in God's presence), while the rich man was in hell (v. 23). We also see that there was no middle ground or purgatory nor any way for a person to switch from one area to the other.

9. Does sending a person to hell for not believing in Jesus sound harsh? Why or why not? (Note: This subject will be discussed in further detail in Session 6.)

10. Why do you think other views about where a person goes in the afterlife have grown in popularity in recent years? What do these views reveal about public interest in the afterlife?

What Now?

11. What further study do you feel like you need in order to better understand what the Bible says about the afterlife?

12. What issues do you feel you need to settle regarding your afterlife beliefs?

SESSION 4

13. With whom do you feel the need to talk regarding the subject of life after death?

Consider This

Select the choice that best represents your opinion right now regarding the following statements:

14. I believe various views of the afterlife . . .
    A. cannot be proven. They are all based on faith and speculation.
    B. show that something exists beyond this life, but nothing more.
    C. are important to understand since the Bible communicates that the choices we make in this life determine where we spend eternity.
    D. I'm not sure what I believe about the afterlife.
    E. OTHER: _____

15. If another person does not share a biblical view of heaven and hell...
    A. I feel the need to share what God's Word says on the issue.
    B. I'm fine letting others believe what they want about the future.
    C. I'm not sure I even know what I believe about the afterlife, much less what to tell someone else.
    D. OTHER: _____

Does Satan Really Exist?

Getting Started

What do *The Simpsons*, *Supernatural*, *South Park*, *Charmed*, and *The Collector* have in common? Each television show mentions or features a version of the being the Bible calls Satan.

In politics, certain leaders from Iran and other nations refer to the US as the Great Satan and to Israel as the Little Satan. In literature, notable authors like Dante, William Blake, and Nathaniel Hawthorne depict Satan as a character in their writings.

In video games, Satan or Satanic images are increasing commonly, such as in *Spawn: Armageddon*, the popular *Doom* series, and the more recent *Guitar Hero III*. In *Guitar Hero III: Legends of Rock*, for instance, Satan is the final boss and goes by the name Lou. He serves as a dark agent for the band in the game's storyline. The game even ends with a rock-version of "The Devil Went Down to Georgia."

But does Satan even exist? How can we know? If he does, is he the Halloween character we see at department stores, dark but harmless, or something more sinister?

Could Satan resemble what we see in classic horror films such as *The Exorcist*, full of evil toward humans? Or is Satan possibly just a creation of the imagination, exported into culture as a symbol of all that is wrong?

In the Bible, Satan goes by several names—"the devil," "the serpent," and even "the dragon." How literal are these names? In a day of science and factual knowledge, does anyone still believe in a personal, spiritual being who fights against us behind the scenes?

This also leads to the question, should Satan be feared? It all depends on who he is. If he's just a myth, then maybe not. But if he's really the leader of spiritual forces that exist in the supernatural realm, then that's another story.

According to research by the Barna Group, six out of ten Americans reject the existence of Satan, indicating that they believe Satan is only a symbol of evil. Yet fifty-four percent of this same group of people believes a person can be influenced by evil spiritual forces such as demons.[20] Clearly, there is much misunderstanding and much disagreement about what people think about Satan.

In this session, we'll explore whether Satan really does exist, what the Bible says on this issue, and how Satan factors into our discussion of suffering and evil.

Talk about It

1. What did you think about Satan as a child? What were the early influences on your thinking?

2. What do you think your coworkers or classmates would say they believe about the existence of Satan? If you have discussed this issue with someone close to you, what did that person say?

3. Why do you think it is important to discover whether Satan really exists?

Here's What I'm Thinking

Satanology 101

Believe it or not, theologians term the research of Satan "Satanology." A brief look at the Bible's discussion of Satan includes the following:

- *He exists*—He is mentioned in seven books of the Old Testament and by every New Testament writer as a real spiritual being.
- *He is a spiritual being*—He is considered the leader of fallen angels.
- *He has a personality*—His personality includes intelligence (2 Corinthians 11:3), emotions (Revelation 12:17), anger (Luke 22:31), and a will (2 Timothy 2:26).
- *He is a liar*—Several biblical verses mention this

fact, such as Ephesians 4:14, 1 Timothy 4:1–4, and 2 Thessalonians 2:10.

(A complete biblical evaluation of Satanology can be found at bible.org keyword "Satanology.")

4. How does the biblical information compare to what you thought about Satan growing up? What are some of the major differences you noticed?

5. What difference does it make to you that Jesus and many other biblical writers mention Satan as a real spiritual being? What additional evidence for Satan's existence would be helpful to you?

Jesus and the Devil in Dialogue

Matthew 4:1–11 shares an encounter between Jesus and Satan. (This same event is also recorded in Luke 4:1–13.)

Then Jesus was led by the Spirit into the desert to be tempted by the devil. After fasting forty days and forty nights, he was hungry. The tempter came to him and said, "If you are the Son of God, tell these stones to become bread."

Jesus answered, "It is written: 'Man does not live on bread alone, but on every word that comes from the mouth of God.'"

Then the devil took him to the holy city and had him stand on the highest point of the temple. "If you are the Son of God," he said, "throw yourself down. For it is written:

" 'He will command his angels concerning you,
and they will lift you up in their hands,
so that you will not strike your foot against a
stone.' "

Jesus answered him, "It is also written: 'Do not put the Lord your God to the test.' "

Again, the devil took him to a very high mountain and showed him all the kingdoms of the world and their splendor. "All this I will give you," he said, "if you will bow down and worship me."

Jesus said to him, "Away from me, Satan! For it is written: 'Worship the Lord your God, and serve him only.' "

Then the devil left him, and angels came and attended him.

SESSION 5

6. What three temptations did Jesus face in His encounter with Satan? How are these temptations similar to issues we face in our lives?

7. How did Jesus respond to each temptation He faced? How does His response show us how we can respond to temptation in our own lives?

The Names of Satan (and Why They Matter)

The following are names of Satan and why they matter:[21]

Name	Purpose	Location
Lucifer	Indicates he was an angel and is a spiritual being	Isaiah 14:12
Ruler of the Demons	Notes his role as a leader	Matthew 12:24
God of This World	Notes his role and power	2 Corinthians 4:4
Devil/Accuser	Highlights his work as a tempter	Matthew 4:1
Prince of the Power of the Air	Notes his role, that he is a being, that he is real	Ephesians 2:2

Name	Purpose	Location
Roaring Lion	Reveals both his power and his attitude	1 Peter 5:8
Serpent	Notes cunning	Genesis 3:1
Dragon	Notes his power and evil	Revelation 12:9
Adversary	Highlights his role as being against those who follow God	Job 1
Tempter	Notes his work toward humans	Matthew 4:3
Anointed Cherub	Points out his previous role as a powerful angel	Ezekiel 28:14
Beelzebub	Can mean lord of the flies or lord of the dwelling, indicating his position as a leader of evil	Matthew 4:3
Belial	Means worthless. Used by Paul against Satan's work	2 Corinthians 6:15
Wicked/Evil One	Notes his identity and work	Matthew 13:19

SESSION 5

8. What about Satan's power and personality can we piece together based on the names attributed to him in the Bible?

9. What difference does it make to you that Satan is mentioned so many times in the Bible? What do you think the Bible could be communicating by mentioning Satan so frequently?

How Should We Deal with Satan?

Satan is described as a powerful spiritual figure throughout the Bible. However, those who follow Christ are given clear instructions on how to handle this very real spiritual being:

- *Be aware of spiritual battle*—"For our struggle is not against flesh and blood, but against the rulers, against the authorities, against the powers of this dark world and against the spiritual forces of evil in the heavenly realms." (Ephesians 6:12)

- *Walk closely with God*—"Submit yourselves, then, to God. Resist the devil, and he will flee from you. Come near to God and he will come near to you." (James 4:7–8)

- *Use God's Word to resist his temptations*—Just like Jesus did in Matthew 4.

- *Remember that God's power in you is greater*— "The one who is in you is greater than the one who is in the world." (1 John 4:4)

10. Which of the above principles is the easiest for you to believe and apply? Which one is the most difficult?

11. Why do you think God allows Satan to continue to deceive people?

12. In what ways is it inconsistent to claim to be a follower of Christ and yet not believe in Satan's existence?

SESSION 5

What Now?

13. What new insights have the verses and discussion used in this session helped you to discover about the role of Satan? How can you use this information in a specific way in your life?

14. Do you believe it is enough to simply accept that the Bible is God's Word without investigating it for yourself on the issue of Satan's existence? Why or why not?

15. What is a proper balance between acknowledging Satan's power while also living in the confidence of God's greater power in our lives through the Holy Spirit?

Consider This

16. Choose the following aspects about Satan that you currently believe are true (check all that apply):
    ___ Satan is just a myth, not a real being.
    ___ There is no way to know whether Satan really exists or not.
    ___ Satan exists, and his power really concerns me.
    ___ I know God can protect and empower me to resist the temptations provided by Satan.

17. I think that learning about Satan:
    ___ Is unnecessary.
    ___ Is helpful to an extent.
    ___ Can be valuable for the spiritual struggles I face in life.
    ___ Is important since he is frequently mentioned in the Bible.

18. Believing in the existence of Satan:
    ___ Helps me to better understand the evil that exists in our world.
    ___ Doesn't help me much in everyday life.
    Reminds me of spiritual battles that occur around
    ___ me as I make daily decisions.
    ___ Affirms the biblical truth of his existence.

How Could God Really Send Anyone to Hell?

Getting Started

For many people, it is difficult to imagine that God could really send anyone to hell. Why would He? If He's loving, wouldn't He let everyone into heaven?

For others, the issue is perspective. "I've attended church my entire life, given money to those in need, and taken a stand for what is right. I've never cheated on my taxes or my spouse. Why wouldn't God let me in?"

Still others think, whether because of God's love or due to our human efforts, that God would make it easy for us to spend eternity with Him. At the very least, He would keep us from suffering for eternity, wouldn't He?

But what if God's love includes punishment for those who don't choose His way to heaven? And what if our positive contributions in this life don't add up to enough points to pay the admission fee into God's presence?

Sure, we're not perfect. Nobody is. But isn't trying our best enough?

Some have suggested that there is no hell, an idea we tackled in an earlier session. But to believe with certainty that hell doesn't exist is quite a gamble. If we're wrong, we could be in big trouble.

One article put it this way,

> I see their point. After all, we talk about a loving, wise, all-powerful Creator who started this whole experiment called life in the first place. If He really does have attributes of compassion in Him, why condemn people to a place of eternal torment? If you were in charge of the universe, wouldn't something like 'remove Hell' be on the top of your list of things to do? Maybe we could make it so people could find a 'get out of hell free' card on E-bay, or better yet put the whole idea of eternal punishment up for a vote.[22]

We'll each find out for sure at some point, but should we wait until it's too late to do anything about it to check? If there was reliable information available right now about how to avoid hell and enter heaven, wouldn't you want it?

"Despite the secularization of American society throughout the 20th and early 21st centuries, Americans themselves seem to be increasingly spiritual. While belief in God has always remained high, contemplation and exploration of some other aspects of spirituality seem to be on an upward trend."
—2004 Gallup survey[23]

In this session, we'll address some of the common concerns people have regarding the issue of a loving God who
would send anyone to hell. In the process, we'll discover that
not only does the Bible talk about hell; it also shares why it
exists and how to avoid it, using very clear terms that can be
applied to our lives and to those around us.

Talk about It

1. In what ways do people commonly mention the
   concept of hell in our culture? Why do you think
   people discuss hell in these ways?

2. Why do you think many people deny that hell even
   exists? What do you think leads people to this
   perspective?

Here's What I'm Thinking

What Famous People Have Said about Hell

People have a tremendous variety of perspectives about hell
and who goes there. Here are a few, ranging from humorous
to serious, from famous voices throughout history on this
issue:

"Each of us bears his own hell." —Virgil

SESSION 6

"Hell is empty and all the devils are here."
—William Shakespeare

"I do not myself feel that any person who is really profoundly human can believe in everlasting punishment. . . . I must say that I think all this doctrine, that hellfire is a punishment for sin, is a doctrine of cruelty."
—Bertrand Russell, in *Why I Am Not a Christian*

Yet these viewpoints are much different than what the Bible tells us regarding the reality and definition of hell and who goes there.

"Only thirty-two percent of those surveyed in a 2002 poll believe hell exists."
—2002 Gallup Survey[24]

What the Bible Says about Hell

Several different terms are used to describe hell in the Bible as can be seen in the following chart:[25]

Biblical Terms Referring to Hell		
Hades	The dwelling place of the wicked dead	Used 11 times in New Testament
Tartaros	Home of wicked angels	Jude 6-7
Lake of Fire	The second death	Revelation 20:15 (5 times in Revelation)

Biblical Terms Referring to Hell		
Bottomless Pit (some translations "the Abyss")	The lower regions as the home of demons	Revelation 9:1 (used 6 times in Revelation)
Gehenna	Place where children were sacrificed to Molech in fire	Jeremiah 7:31; Matthew 23:33
Outer Darkness	Place where there is weeping and gnashing of teeth	Matthew 8:12; 22:13; 25:30
Place of Torment	Used in same context as Hades	Luke 16:28
Fiery Furnace	Place angels will throw evildoers	Matthew 13:42
Everlasting Destruction	Place those who do not know God will be sent	2 Thessalonians 1:8-9
Eternal Punishment	Place Jesus says the wicked will go	Matthew 25:46
Exclusion from God's Presence	The result of each of the above	John 16:11

3. How do you think some of the well-known people quoted above came up with their opinions about hell? How is this similar to how you developed your thoughts on hell? How is it different?

4. Review some of the names given for hell above. (As
time allows, look up a few of the corresponding
verses from the Bible and read these names within
their context.) What do these names communicate
about what hell is like? In what ways do these
descriptions fit your previous conceptions of what
hell is like? How are they different?

 How did Jesus describe hell (called "hades" in some
translations) in Luke 16:19–24? What was hell like
for the rich man who was there after his death? How
long did it take for him to get there after he died?

Non-Biblical Viewpoints of Hell

Some of the common non-biblical viewpoints of hell include:

* *Hell does not exist*—"There is no such place.
  Christians just made it up."
* *Hell is the suffering we experience on earth*—"Hell
  is what you go through on earth."
* *Hell is simply to cease to exist upon death
  (annihilation)*—"It refers to the final destruction of
  all evil persons."
* *Hell is temporary*—"All persons will ultimately be
  saved."

6. Which of the above viewpoints is the most common among people you know? Which is least common?

7. If someone asks you why you believe in hell, how would you respond? What verses from the Bible would be most helpful in your explanation? What could you say to someone who did not believe the Bible?

How to Avoid Hell (and Help Others Avoid it, Too!)

Fortunately, hell is not the only option. Most people don't like to hear it stated this way, but God never sends people to hell. He has designed a plan for us to spend eternity with Him, but it requires that we place our faith and trust in Him.

The reason it is important to explain the reality and ugliness of hell is to help us understand our need to avoid it. If hell is a place of permanent pain and suffering, why wouldn't we want to avoid it? If God has offered another option that leads to joyful eternity with Him, where do we sign up?

The reason many people miss out on God's way to heaven is simple—they aren't looking for it. Even those who are often assume there must be a series of steps or good deeds to accomplish in order to make the cut.

But for those who seek God, He has revealed the way to Him through His Son, Jesus Christ. What did Jesus say about avoiding hell and spending eternity with God?

- **God <u>wants</u> us to spend eternity with Him**—*"For God so loved the world that he gave his one and only Son, that whoever believes in him shall not perish but have eternal life."* (John 3:16)

- **God has provided <u>a way</u> to spend eternity with Him by grace through faith**—*"For it is by grace you have been saved, through faith—and this not from yourselves, it is the gift of God—not by works, so that no one can boast."* (Ephesians 2:8–9)

- **God has provided only <u>one way</u> to enter heaven**—*"I am the way and the truth and the life. No one comes to the Father except through me."* (John 14:6)

  "Salvation is found in no one else, for there is no other name under heaven given to men by which we must be saved." (Acts 4:12)

- **God has provided the Bible so we could have <u>confidence</u> of our eternal life**—*"God has given us eternal life, and this life is in his Son. He who has the Son has life; he who does not have the Son of God does not have life. I write these things to you who believe in the name of the Son of God so that you may know that you have eternal life."* (1 John 5:11–13)

8. How does it make you feel to hear that God desires for us to spend eternity with Him? How is this

perspective different from how many people view God?

9. Do you think it seems narrow-minded for God to provide only one way to spend eternity with Him? Why or why not?

10. If getting into heaven was based on our performance, how would a person know if he or she had done enough to make it?

11. Why is the Bible important to use in sharing the good news that a person can have eternal life with God? How would you approach talking about eternal life differently with someone who was antagonistic toward the Bible?

Does God Care Where We Spend Eternity?

The Bible says that even before we were born, God loved us and desired to have a personal relationship with us. As a result, He chose to make it possible for us to know Him. Romans 5:8 explains that, "God demonstrates his own love for us in this: While we were still sinners, Christ died for us."

What does this mean? It tells us that God not only loves us, but provided a way for us to know Him long before we were even born. Why do Christians believe that the death and resurrection of Jesus Christ is of central importance to Christianity? Because without Christ's death on our behalf, we are sinners who have no access to God. No amount of positive efforts we perform will be enough to cover our sins.

A powerful example is found in the scene of Jesus on the cross. He was crucified between two criminals who were sentenced to death for their crimes. One of the men mocked Jesus and told Him to get down from the cross if He was really God's son, the Messiah.

The other man, however, had a more humble attitude. He understood he would soon die. He knew Jesus claimed to be God's Son. So he made a request.

His solitary wish can be found in one sentence in the Gospel of Luke. "Jesus, remember me when you come into your kingdom" (Luke 23:42).

How did Jesus respond? We are told that Jesus answered, "I tell you the truth, today you will be with me in paradise" (Luke 23:43).

That was it. This dying criminal had no time to change his habits, give to the poor, or even be baptized. He could only ask Jesus to take him into His kingdom.

Jesus called it paradise. That's exactly what heaven is. Getting there does not require a passport, a certain sum of money, or a spectacular level of achievement. It only requires Jesus.

12. How is the request by the man on the cross similar to how God requires us to come to Him in our lives?

13. Though eternal life with God is through faith, what happens to our lives when we choose to follow Christ?

14. Do you believe a person can know for certain he or she will go to heaven? Why or why not?

15. How does knowing that a person will spend eternity in heaven make it easier to handle the suffering and evil in our world? How does it help you personally?

What Now?

16. What information in this session has been the most helpful in providing understanding of the relationship God desires to have with us?

17. Which portion of this session do you think will be most useful in discussing your faith with another person?

18. What information do you still desire to learn in the process of better understanding how a person can have a relationship with God and eternal life in heaven?

Consider This

Answer the following belief statements based on your discussion in this session:

19. I believe heaven and hell are two very real places and that every person will ultimately go to one place or the other.
___ True
___ False
___ Not sure

20. I believe it is possible to know for sure that I have eternal life with God in heaven:
___ True
___ False
___ Not sure

21. I believe that there is only one way to heaven— through Jesus Christ:
___ True
___ False
___ Not sure

22. I believe it is critical to share the way to God through Jesus Christ with others to help as many people as possible spend eternity in heaven:
___ True
___ False
___ Not sure

23. Having completed this series, I would like to do the following. (Mark all that apply.):
___ Become a believer in Christ.
___ Recommit my life to loving and serving Christ.
___ Begin a regular time of Bible reading and study.
___ Continue with another title in the Contenders series (such as *How Is Christianity Different from Other Religions?*).
___ Lead a similar study with some of my friends, coworkers, classmates, or family.

SESSION 6

End your final session in a brief time of silent prayer regarding your next step in your spiritual journey. Afterwards, decide as a group what to do next in your desire to continue your spiritual growth.

"I could never myself believe in God, if it were not for the cross. . . . In the real world of pain, how could one worship a God who was immune to it?" —John Stott[26]

Also, don't forget to look at the "Additional Resources" section for audio, videos, Internet materials, and books on this issue that can be used personally or as additional group learning tools. In addition, we have provided two appendices for your reference. The first is for those who would like to begin a relationship with God. The second is an outline of Bible verses to help you in praying for other people who have yet to experience the joy of a personal relationship with Christ.

Finally, please have a representative from your group take a moment to send an email to the Contenders series website (www.contendersseries.com) to share highlights from your group with others. We would appreciate any stories of life-change that can be used to encourage others in their spiritual journey. God bless you as you continue growing in your spiritual journey!

APPENDIX A:

How to Begin a Personal Relationship with God

If you would like to begin a personal relationship with God that promises joy, forgiveness, and eternal life, you can do so right now by doing the following:

1. Believe that God exists and that He sent His Son Jesus Christ in human form to Earth (John 3:16; Romans 10:9).
2. Accept God's free gift of new life through the death and resurrection of God's only son, Jesus Christ (Ephesians 2:8–9).
3. Commit to following God's plan for your life (1 Peter 1:21–23; Ephesians 2:1–7).
4. Determine to make Jesus Christ the ultimate leader and final authority of your life (Matthew 7:21–27; 1 John 4:15).

There is no magic formula or special prayer to begin your relationship with God. However, the following prayer is one that can be used to accept God's free gift of salvation through Jesus Christ by faith:

> "Dear Lord Jesus, I admit that I have
> sinned. I know I cannot save myself. Thank
> You for dying on the cross and taking my
> place. I believe that Your death was for me
> and receive Your sacrifice on my behalf. I
> transfer all of my trust from myself and turn
> all of my desires over to You. I open the door
> of my life to You and by faith receive You as
> my Savior and Lord, making You the ultimate
> Leader of my life. Thank You for forgiving
> my sins and giving me eternal life. Amen."

If you have made this decision, congratulations! You have just made the greatest commitment of your life. As a new follower of Jesus, you will have many questions, and this group is a great place to begin. Let your group leaders know about your decision and ask what resources they have available to assist you in your new spiritual adventure.

Other ways you can grow in your new relationship with God include:

- spending regular time in prayer and Bible reading.
- finding a Bible-teaching church where you can grow with other followers of Christ.
- seeking opportunities to tell others about Jesus through acts of service and everyday conversations.

For more information on growing in your relationship with God, please see www.contendersseries.com or www.johnankerberg.org. You can also receive additional materials by contacting the authors at:

The Ankerberg Theological Research Institute
P.O. Box 8977
Chattanooga, TN 37414
Phone: (423) 892-7722

APPENDIX B:

Praying for Those Who Do Not Believe

The Scriptures provide several ways for us to pray for those who do not know Jesus. However, it's often a daunting task to choose where to begin in praying for others. The following outline of verses is designed to assist in offering biblical prayers for those who do not believe.

1. Pray for God to draw the person to Himself.

   No one can come to me unless the Father who sent me draws him. (John 6:44)

2. Pray that the person would desire God.

   But in their distress they turned to the LORD, the God of Israel, and sought him, and he was found by them. (2 Chronicles 15:4)

   God did this so that men would seek him and perhaps reach out for him and find him, though he is not far from each one of us. (Acts 17:27)

3. Pray for an understanding and acceptance of God's Word.

   Consequently, faith comes from hearing the message, and the message is heard through the word of Christ. (Romans 10:17)

   And we also thank God continually because, when you received the word of God, which you heard from us, you accepted it not as the word of men, but as it actually is, the word of God, which is at work in you who believe. (1 Thessalonians 2:13)

4. Pray that Satan would not blind them.

   When anyone hears the message about the kingdom and does not understand it, the evil one comes and snatches away what was sown in his heart. (Matthew 13:19)

   The god of this age has blinded the minds of unbelievers, so that they cannot see the light of the gospel of the glory of Christ, who is the image of God. (2 Corinthians 4:4)

5. Pray that the Holy Spirit would convict of sin.

   When he comes, he will convict the world of guilt in regard to sin and righteousness and judgment. (Matthew 16:8)

6. Pray for someone to share Christ with them.

   Ask the Lord of the harvest, therefore, to send out workers into his harvest field. (Matthew 9:38)

7. Pray that God provides His grace and repentance. (Repentance is a change of mind that leads to changed behavior.)

*Repent, then, and turn to God, so that your sins
may be wiped out, that times of refreshing may come
from the Lord.* (Acts 3:19)

*For it is by grace you have been saved, through
faith—and this not from yourselves, it is the gift
of God—not by works, so that no one can boast.*
(Ephesians 2:8–9)

8. Pray that they believe and entrust themselves in Jesus
    as Savior.

    *Yet to all who received him, to those who believed
    in his name, he gave the right to become children of
    God.* (John 1:12)

    *I tell you the truth, whoever hears my word and
    believes him who sent me has eternal life and will
    not be condemned; he has crossed over from death
    to life.* (John 5:24)

9. Pray that they confess Jesus as Lord.

    *That if you confess with your mouth, "Jesus is
    Lord," and believe in your heart that God raised him
    from the dead, you will be saved. For it is with your
    heart that you believe and are justified, and it is with
    your mouth that you confess and are saved.* (Romans
    10:9–10)

10. Pray that they continue to grow spiritually and learn
    how to surrender all to follow Jesus.

    *Then Jesus said to his disciples, "If anyone would
    come after me, he must deny himself and take up his
    cross and follow me."* (Matthew 16:24)

    *"But whatever was to my profit I now consider
    loss for the sake of Christ. What is more, I consider*

everything a loss compared to the surpassing greatness of knowing Christ Jesus my Lord, for whose sake I have lost all things. I consider them rubbish, that I may gain Christ. (Philippians 3:7–8)

So then, just as you received Christ Jesus as Lord, continue to live in him, rooted and built up in him, strengthened in the faith as you were taught, and overflowing with thankfulness. (Colossians 2:6–7)

Additional Resources

Interested in learning more? For those seriously pursuing more on the life of Christ and Christianity, several additional quality tools exist. We have listed below several other resources available from The Ankerberg Theological Research Institute along with a list of helpful websites on the subject.

Ankerberg Theological Research Institute Resources

All of the following Ankerberg resources can be ordered online at www.johnankerberg.org or by phone at (423) 892-7722.

Books

All of the following books are authored or coauthored by Dr. John Ankerberg or Dillon Burroughs:

Ready with An Answer for the Tough Questions About God (Eugene, OR: Harvest House, 1997).

The Case for Jesus the Messiah: Incredible Prophecies that Prove God Exists (Chattanooga, TN: Ankerberg Theological Research Institute, 1989).

Defending Your Faith (Chattanooga, TN: AMG Publishers, 2007).

Fast Facts on Defending Your Faith (Eugene, OR: Harvest House, 2002).

The Facts on Why You Can Believe the Bible (Eugene, OR: Harvest House, 2004).

Knowing the Truth About the Reliability of the Bible (Eugene, OR: Harvest House, 1997).

Video and Audio Programs & Transcripts

The following topics are available in VHS & DVD format. Most programs offer downloadable transcripts as well.

Dealing with Doubts

The Problem of Evil: Why Does God Allow Evil and Suffering in the World?

Why Do Bad Things Happen to Good People?

Online Articles & Video Downloads

Over 2,500 online articles and video downloads on Christianity and comparative religions are hosted on The Ankerberg Theological Research Institute website. For an A to Z directory, see http://www.johnankerberg.org/Articles/archives-ap.htm.

About the Authors

Dr. John Ankerberg is host of the award-winning apologetics TV and radio program *The John Ankerberg Show*, which is broadcast in more than 185 countries. Founder and president of the Ankerberg Theological Research Institute, John has authored more than sixty books, including the bestselling *Facts On* apologetics series, with over 2 million copies in print, and *Defending Your Faith* (AMG Publishers). His training includes three earned degrees: a Master of Arts in church history and the philosophy of Christian thought, a Master of Divinity from Trinity Evangelical Divinity School, and a Doctor of Ministry from Luther Rice Seminary. For more information, see www.johnankerberg.org.

Dillon Burroughs is a research associate for the Ankerberg Theological Research Institute. Author or coauthor of numerous books, including *Defending Your Faith* (AMG Publishers), *What's the Big Deal About Jesus?*, and *Comparing Christianity with World Religions*, Dillon is a graduate of Dallas Theological Seminary and lives in Tennessee with his wife, Deborah, and two children.

Endnotes

1   These guidelines adapted from Judson Poling, *How Reliable Is the Bible?*, rev. ed., (Grand Rapids, MI: Zondervan, 2003), pp. 14–15.

2   Erwin Lutzer, *Where Was God? Answers to Tough Questions About God and Natural Disasters* (Wheaton, IL: Tyndale, 2006), p. 6.

3   Albert Mohler, "Facing the Reality of Evil," *On Faith*, April 2007. Accessed at http://newsweek.washingtonpost.com/onfaith/r_albert_mohler_jr/2007/04/facing_the_reality_of_evil.html.

4   Statistics from the Family Prevention Fund website, http://www.endabuse.org/resources/facts/.

5   Lutzer, *Where Was God?* p. 83.

6   Nigel Wight, *The Satan Syndrome* (Grand Rapids, MI: Zondervan, 1990), p. 66.

7   Adapted from the article by Norman Geisler, "The Problem of Evil—Part Two," The Ankerberg Theological Research Association. Accessed at http://www.johnankerberg.org/Articles/theological-dictionary/TD1199W1.htm._

8   John Stott, *The Cross of Christ* (Downers Grove, IL: InterVarsity Press, 1986), p. 311.

9   Charlie Campbell, "If God, Why Evil and Suffering?" AlwaysBeReady.com. Accessed at http://www.alwaysbeready.com/images/library/campbell-charlie/studies-topical/whyevil/whyevil-a.htm.

10   Ken Boa and Larry Moody, *I'm Glad You Asked* (Colorado Springs, CO: Victor, 1982, 1994), p. 136.

11   Philip Yancey, *Disappointment with God* (Grand Rapids, MI: Zondervan), pp. 179–181.

12   Elie Wiesel, *Night* (New York: Bantam), pp. 75–75, quoted in W. Aldrich, *When God Was Taken Captive* (Sisters, OR: Multnomah, 1989), pp. 19–41.

13   C.S. Lewis, *The Problem of Pain* (San Francisco, CA: HarperOne, 1962), p. 93.

14   Billy Graham, *The Billy Graham Worker's Handbook* (Minneapolis, MN: Worldwide Publications, 1984), p. 223.

15   All verses in this chart are from the New American Standard Bible.

16   "Americans Describe their Views about Life after Death," Barna Group, October 21, 2003. Accessed at http://www.barna.org/FlexPage.aspx?Page=BarnaUpdate&BarnaUpdateID=150.

17   David L. Hocking, "What We Believe," *The Biola Hour Guidelines* (La Mirada, CA: Biola University, 1982), pp. 11–14. Accessed at http://www.bible.org/illus.php?topic_id=715.

18   Bruce Bickel and Stan Jantz, *Bible Answers to Life's Big Questions* (Eugene, OR: Harvest House, 2006), p. 158.

19   C.S. Lewis, *The Problem of Pain* (San Francisco, CA: HarperOne, 1962), p. 107.

20   "Americans Draw Theological Beliefs from Diverse Points of View," *The Barna Update,* October 8, 2002. Accessed at http://www.barna.org/FlexPage.aspx?Page=BarnaUpdate&BarnaUpdateID=122.

21   Thanks to AllaboutGod.com for the information used to compile this chart. See http://www.allaboutgod.com/names-of-satan-faq.htm.

22   Lane Palmer, "How Could a Loving God Send Anyone to Hell?" *Dare2Share.org*, January, 13, 2004. Accessed at http://www.dare2share.org/devotions/how-could-a-loving-god-send-anyone-to-hell.

23   Albert L. Winseman, "Eternal Destinations: Americans Believe in Heaven, Hell," *Gallup*, May 25, 2004. Accessed at http://www.gallup.com/poll/11770/Eternal-Destinations-Americans-Believe-Heaven-Hell.aspx.

24   Joseph Mazzuca, "Britons Look on the Bright Side of Afterlife," *Gallup*, October 22, 2002. Accessed at http://www.gallup.com/poll/7045/Britons-Look-Bright-Side-Afterlife.aspx.

25   For more on these names for hell, see our study in Lesson 9 of *Defending Your Faith* (Chattanooga, TN: AMG Publishers, 2007).

26   John Stott, *The Cross of Christ* (Downers Grove, IL: InterVarsity Press, 1986), pp. 335–336.

About the Ankerberg Theological Research Institute

Asking tough questions...Offering real answers

Mission Statement
The Ankerberg Theological Research Institute (ATRI) is a Christian media organization designed to investigate and answer today's critical questions concerning issues of spirituality, popular culture, and comparative religions.

> *But in your hearts set apart Christ as Lord.*
> *Always be prepared to give an answer to*
> *everyone who asks you to give the reason*
> *for the hope that you have. But do this*
> *with gentleness and respect, keeping a*
> *clear conscience, so that those who speak*
> *maliciously against your good behavior in*
> *Christ may be ashamed of their slander.*
> (1 Peter 3:15–16)

ATRI utilizes five strategies to accomplish this mission:

> *The John Ankerberg Show*—Our weekly half-hour
> TV program reaches over 147 million people in
> the US, in addition to millions more worldwide via

satellite. The award-winning *John Ankerberg Show* is considered the longest-running and most established television program available today providing answers to issues of importance to Christians (also called Apologetics). Its documentary specials have been featured as nationwide television specials.

ATRI Radio—ATRI reaches thousands of people through its weekend one-hour program and new one-minute daily radio commentary that is being offered on over 100 stations nationwide.

JohnAnkerberg.org: ATRI's Web site reaches nearly three million unique visitors per year from 184 countries, providing a truly global impact. ATRI continues to utilize today's newest media formats as well, including online audio and video downloads, podcasts, blogs, and mobile technologies.

ATRI Resources: In addition to over 84 combined published books and 2.5 million books sold by ATRI authors in several languages, its resources include over 2,500 online articles that have been utilized as research by some of today's best known media and academic organizations, both Christian and mainstream. In addition, ATRI offers transcripts of its TV interviews, which include thousands of hours of material from the past 28 years with top religious scholars.

ATRI Events: Past speaking engagements have included Promise Keepers events, Focus on the Family seminars, and the National Apologetics Conference. Founder Dr. John Ankerberg has personally spoken to over one million people during his speaking engagements and seminars in dozens of countries spanning five continents.

Due to advanced research and long-standing work, founder and president Dr. John Ankerberg is regularly quoted in both Christian and mainstream media including NBC, ABC, Daystar, and INSP, and has even testified before the U.S. Congressional Sub-Committee on financial accountability for Christian non-profit organizations. A board member for many Christian media organizations, Dr. Ankerberg also serves on the board of directors for the National Religious Broadcasters Association.

CONTENDERS BIBLE STUDY SERIES

Questions about God, Christianity, and the Bible aren't going away. How will you respond?

The challenging uncertainties in your mind, or in the mind of someone you know, are worth taking time to explore. In six engaging sessions designed to get small groups talking, each guide in the Contenders Bible Study Series™ deals head-on with some of the controversies commonly asked about Christianity.

How Do We Know God Exists?
(ISBN-13: 978-089957781-4) 5.5" x 8.5"
Paperback / 112 pages

Why Does God Allow Suffering and Evil?
(ISBN-13: 978-089957782-1) 5.5" x 8.5"
Paperback / 112 pages

How Do We Know the Bible Is True?
(ISBN-13: 978-089957779-1) 5.5" x 8.5"
Paperback / 112 pages

How Is Christianity Different from Other Religions?
(ISBN-13: 978-089957780-7) 5.5" x 8.5"
Paperback / 112 pages